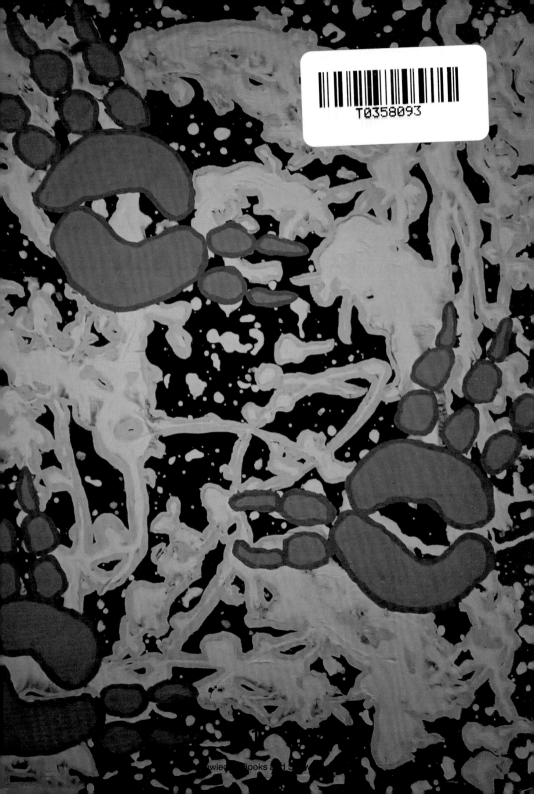

A long time ago lived a small boy whose parents had died. He moved and camped with his mean relatives. They would not give him much food or water. One day, everyone except the boy was out hunting and gathering. While the relatives were gone, he drank all the water. When the relatives returned, they were thirsty but had nothing to drink. In anger, they hit the boy and hurt him. He ran away and climbed a tall tree and made himself into a soft, furry koala. All he needed now were leaves and not water. He stayed high and safe where no-one could hurt him again.

Knowledge Books and Software

3

When only the First Peoples lived in Australia, there were millions of koalas. Since then, lots of people have arrived from around the world and built roads and cities. The new people did not know about koalas. They wondered what to name these animals. Some people called them monkey bears. They climbed like a monkey and looked like a bear. They asked the Dharug people of Sydney what to call them. They gave them the name 'koala' which means 'no water' in the Dharug language.

Knowledge Books and Software

Koalas are important to the First Peoples of Eastern Australia. Some people had them as a totem animal not to be eaten. To others, they were an important type of food. The people only took what they needed to eat. Different groups have different names for the koala. In this book, I call them burabi because I live in Bundjalung country. In Jagera you say, *dumbirrbi*. In Yugarabul you say, *marrambi*. In Wiradjuri, you say, *barandang*.

Knowledge Books and Software

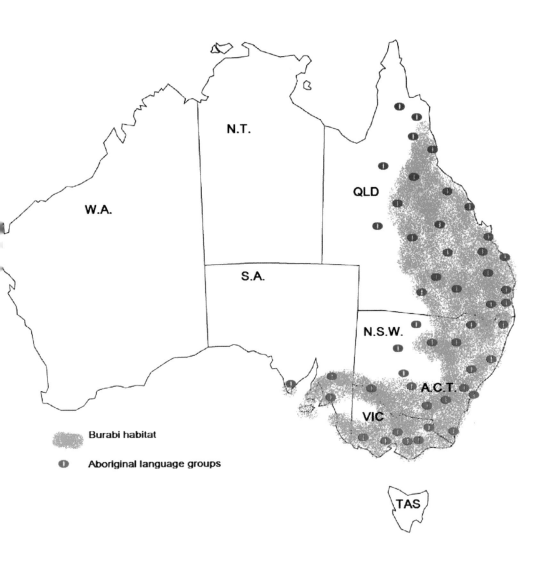

Burabi habitat

Aboriginal language groups

First Nations people are alert to the animals and plants. They watch and learn from burabi. They learn about caring for children from the way burabi care for joeys. Small joeys stay safe inside the mum's pouch. When bigger, they ride on mum's tummy or back. When even bigger, they leave mum and find new trees to make their home. I used to have a job at a First People's place. It has the burabi mascot on its sign. My friend Greg started this place. He is an Aboriginal and Islander man. The burabi is like his special totem animal, so he protects them. This group helps Aboriginal and Islander families to care about each other and their children, just like burabi do.

Knowledge Books and Software

Burabi are good at climbing. You can practise climbing too. Try to always have at least one hand and one foot on something. Burabi carry their small joeys around to protect them. I used to carry my baby son in a carrier, and he loved it. You can try to protect and love those in your family too. Burabi sleep a lot to stay healthy and grow. You too can try to get plenty of sleep at night to stay healthy and grow strong.

Knowledge Books and Software

People around the world know and love burabi. Did you know a koala called *Borobi* was the life-size mascot for the Gold Coast Games? This was in 2018 on the Gold Coast. *Borobi* means koala. He has First Nations' art on his hands and feet. *Borobi* is still busy seeing people. You can learn more about what *Borobi* does at his webpage.

Knowledge Books and Software

13

Just up the road from my house is an area called Koala Beach. Many burabi live there. It is safe for them because dogs and cats are not allowed. Everyone drives slowly and carefully. All the houses have burabi food trees around them or in their yards. People check on local burabi often to make sure they are healthy and safe. At night you can hear the burabi grunting loudly in the trees. You can see them walking along the ground to find a new tree.

Knowledge Books and Software

KOALA BEACH

DOGS AND CATS ARE NOT PERMITTED TEMPORARILY OR PERMANENTLY WITHIN KOALA BEACH ESTATE
Penalties Apply

SEC 14.1h, 20.1b OF THE COMPANION ANIMALS ACT 1998
SEC 632 OF THE LOCAL GOVERNMENT ACT 1993

TWEED SHIRE COUNCIL

Burabi face some dangers to their health and lives. One is bushfires. Many burabi die from being burned. Bushfires destroy much of the bush, leaving little or no food. The forest can take up to 10 years to recover from a big bushfire. For thousands of years, smart First Peoples used fire in caring for the land. Firestick burning is where small areas are burned regularly in a controlled way. The fire clears bushy areas for hunting and helps new trees and plants grow. Firestick burning stopped big bushfires from happening so burabi were safer.

Knowledge Books and Software

17

Burabi are getting very sick. The sickness can make them go blind. It also stops them having joeys. When their trees are cut down there is less food. The sickness can become worse. If you see a burabi with sore eyes or a brown stained bottom, it is very sick. These burabi need help from a local koala rescue group.

18

In my city, there is a place called **Friends of the Koala**. They rescue sick and injured burabi, and burabi with no mums. Burabi get food and medicine to help them. Then, they are set free into the bush. **Friends of the Koala** fix up koala places and grow koala food trees. **Friends of the Koala** also have a place where people can visit and learn about burabi.

FRIENDS OF THE KOALA INC.

KOALA TOURS
Mon-Fri 10am & 2pm
Sat 10am

www.friendsofthekoala.org

OFFICE
6621 4664
Rifle Range Road

KOALA RESCUE
6622 1233 24 HOUR HOTLINE

Would you like to help burabi? Talk with your family and friends about how you can help. Here are some ideas. You could adopt a burabi through a website such as **www.savethekoala.com**. You could plant a food tree in your backyard. You could go to a forest to plant food trees. You could visit a koala hospital. Keep your dogs and cats away from koalas. If we all help, there will be lots of happy burabi for a long time to come.

Knowledge Books and Software

Word bank

koala	animals
alert	hospital
burabi	important
everyone	different
Jagera	children
Yugambeh	practise
Wiradjuri	bushfires
Dharug	thousands
relatives	rescue
everyone	
climbed	
millions	

Knowledge Books and Software